God Bless America

Glen Fyffe

VANTAGE PRESS
New York

Published by Vantage Press, Inc.
419 Park Ave. South, New York, NY 10016

Manufactured in the United States of America
ISBN: 0-533-14891-X

Library of Congress Catalog Card No.: 2004092083

0 9 8 7 6 5 4 3 2 1

Contents

Acknowledgments

My acknowledgments to my Lord God Almighty, my wife of many years, and my three children, my nieces, nephews, brothers, sister, and to my extended family and friends. God bless. Thanks for your support.

God Bless America

God bless America, a land so vast so great.
Shadowing with mighty wings, stretching from north to
south.
Great planes, great valleys, great hills, and great lakes.
Great rivers run for hundreds of miles,
rivers so wide, and rivers so deep
race to the oceans with mighty force.

Built on unique principles, a land united stands,
a land united with mighty force, echoes to the end of the
earth.

Triumph over seas and skies, all the nations see,
long arms fathom the deepest depths even to the stars.

Bless with health, bless with wealth, all the nations meet,
to partake in a pride so highly esteemed,
where most dreams came true.

The poor and oppressed flee from all nations,
taking refuge under thy wings.

Even from time to time, stand united and free,
singing songs of victories,
a land that God so richly blessed.

Mother Earth

Way out here in the center of the universe
hangs the great bright white and blue,
neighbouring by millions of stars,
most zillions of light years away,
with such distant space between deep echoes deep,
in the silence of eternal dark,
billions of stars twinkle their lights.

Hangs and governs by a mighty hand, eyes not able to see,
Shining queen above all stars, wears the crown of life.
Earth, water, clouds, winds, fire, heated sunshine,
from such combined forces come forth life.
Man, plants, fishes, birds and beasts.

The earth, the world, mother earth.
The mother of life, the birth of all nations.
From her womb issues all generations
great kings, great kingdoms.
The absolute she reclaimed to the crest of her bosom,
The abominate she swallowed up in the dust of her belly
Earth the authentic of our solar system.

In the Presence of the Lord

In the presence of the Lord
all is shine and glorious,
there is supernatural peace
there is unconditional love,
there is virtue, there is life, there is rest,
there is eternal majesties,
there is crown of eternity,
in the presence of the Lord.

In the presence of the Lord,
there is joy, happiness, worship, praise and singing.
There is flowing rivers of living waters,
there are angels seraphim, and cherubim.
There are great multitudes, trumpeth sound,
all nations bow in humble adorations.
There is total triumph of undisputed victory,
there is eternal display of ultimate conclusion of power,
in the presence of the Lord,
in the presence of the Lord.

Pains of Life

How painful for some men for life to live, or just to live their lives. They sow in good hope, yet they reap, in tears even reap what they sow not.

How painful for some men for life to live, when joy said I know you not, so I flew from you and sorrow said, you are my friend I will embrace you and stay with you always.

How painful for some men for life to live, when you are right yet, they say you are wrong, when you do the right they still call it wrong, and when you are really wrong they say that you are double wrong even until death.

How painful for some men for life to live, when in time of their needs I sowed them good seeds and they were happy indeed but in time of my needs they say that I am greedy and did me bad deeds.

How painful for some men for life to live, when eyes we got, but we see not, when feet we got, but we walk not, when hands and fingers we got, but we handles and findles not, when heads we got, but edifieth not, when we are full, but we still hunger and thirst.

How painful for some men for life to live, when we fail to reach out to the higher powers, that turn tears into laughter, sorrows into joy, wrongs turn to right, bad deeds to good seeds, eyes open, feet walks, hands and fingers handles and findles, heads edifieth, and thirsts are quenched.

4

Poverty

I searched the store rooms of wealth,
mine eyes behold its great abundance.
Abundance in gold, abundance in silver,
abundance in diamond and all precious stones.
I saw titles, deeds, great possessions, and ownerships.
Enough for the rich, enough for the poor,
enough for the satisfied,
the greedy, the dishonest, the seller, the buyer,
the kind giver, the humble laborer,
them that want more, more, more and more,
enough for every man.

I asked the store room keeper for my portion,
he replied, go labour with thine hands,
it will come to thee, and so I did,
but, it was not always so.
Instead poverty withstood me,
poverty attacks, poverty robs,
Poverty sends a constant wind blowing away,
rewards for laboring hands.

Poverty lurks in the dark, attacks from behind,
one will never see its face.
Poverty sucks, drains, withers and dries up
the substance of prosperity.

Poverty like a stubborn sore
which deprives a wound from healing,
like wounded feet and broken arms,
so does poverty to the life of an ambitious man.

A river runs wild, yet tamed and rechanneled
to its rightful course.
The hills move to and fro at the
shaking of an earthquake.
In spring times trees bud forth
young and tender leaves flourished in the summer,
in autumn leaves are changed to red, yellow,
ripe or multicolored.
After the devastation of a raging storm
all becomes calm and rebirth takes place,
but poverty has never compromise,
neither change its constant destructive position,
neither give a smile or a sigh of relief.

O that poverty would go its ways,
in the belly of darkness and despair,
and its place of hopelessness and atrocities,
where it belongs.

Poverty loves an empty barn,
it consumes vineyards,
chases the rain clouds with the wind,
shattered dreams, wounded ambitions,
broken the spirit, discredited perseverance.
Poverty shadows lights, the days go dark,
hopes have been broken down,
weakened strength.
O that poverty would go its way
in the belly of darkness and despair,
and its place of hopelessness and atrocities
where it belongs.

Poverty robs the parents,
the children lack necessities,
begging in the rags,
begging in the street,
the cupboard bare, the lack of food,
the rain clouds flee, the sun bares down,
the parched land, the lack of fund,
the hopeless days nights full of fear,
the daily toil yet ends not meet,
the abandoned city the crumbled house.

Behold poverty displays its power
and grips its constant position,
even till the end of time.
O that poverty would go its ways
in the belly of darkness and despair,
and its place of hopelessness
and atrocities where it belongs.

Fly Plane Fly

Fly plane fly, take off to the skies,
by force of mighty thrust,
climb through the clouds.
Higher, higher, higher, and higher.
Speed so fast sound barriers are broken.
View of clouds, rain, lightning and thunder,
way down below.
Shining object shutters across the skies,
far distance, and time, are greatly shrunk.

Fly plane fly, high across the skies,
on wings of lightning, wings of fire
overtake the night, subdue the day
sonic speed like roaring thunder
spans time zones in the twinkle of an eye.
Oceans, continents, seas are bridged,
luxurious liners streak the skies,
with only moments left behind.

Mighty Trucks

From small to medium, large all strong,
trucks on wheels of rolling thunder,
engines with power of hundreds of horses,
trucks for all purposes, different makes and kinds.

With sturdy frame and multi wheels
the burden of man and beast they bear,
laden with necessities the nation needs
in all its great abundance.

Before the day completely past,
the duties of a thousand beasts is done,
instead of a month it takes a day,
where is the burden for a truck to bear
with strength of a thousand horses,
ready to take on greater task.

No green pastures like a horse to graze,
no trees for a truck to shade,
a tank of fuel not a barn of hay,
few cans of oil no barley no corn,
few gallons of water not a running stream,
the needs of trucks is already met.

Help build great cities and span mighty rivers,
Haul the burden of a thousand beasts,
with mighty speed than the quickest steed,
with urgent needs it takes the lead,
with all necessities a nation's need.

Horns of trumpet sounding blast,
make way clear for the dragon roars,
sniff up the wind out puff black smoke,
rumble rumble the ground vibrates,
who can stand in the way of a truck.

Triumph over the steepest hills,
speed and power with lots to spare,
no load too heavy for a truck to bear,
power of fire and a dragon's heart.

Roam the highways day and nights,
city streets and winding roads,
service roads and narrow lanes,
tunnels, bridges, and viaducts,
ceaseless journey carry on.

Villages, great and minor towns,
deep valleys and great plains,
through wilderness and desert sands,
pierce the rain and brake the wind,
plow the snow and splash the mud.

Through deserted places and barren lands,
high floods and rocky roads,
the spawn of death has lost its grip,
appetite for blood deprives,
man and machine in accordance,
run errands with aggressive force.

Roll roll o mighty wheels,
all harvests wait for thee,
roll roll o mighty wheels,
in millions roam the earth,
constant supplies all nations need,
most life depends on thee.

Summer Lust

At the dawn of spring, the winter flees,
its seasonal reign is ended,
packing all its belongings and leaves,
to its place in its master's bosom.

Its cold, snows, and dampy rain
frozen hails and icy wind,
its gray, thick, and heavy dark clouds,
in its bosom it rolls like a scroll.

The sun regains its full domain,
as winter timely departs
the fresh, warm, clear brightness of spring,
ushers in summer with open arms,
as the sun increases its steamy degree.

Summer displaces winter's rugged past,
its legacy dissolves,
the whole wide world claps its hands,
and great rejoicing under the sun.

Winter's garments tucks away,
hair, scales, and feathers sheds,
all new garments light and bright,
nature exposes its beauty and its majesties,
in its naked fashions and forms.

As the glow that summer displays unfolds,
the dynamics of all life rise to high peak,
with ceaseless urge for summers, fun,
the lust of the eyes beams to the heart,
the heart emotionalizes the urge,
all lust for what seems good in the eyes,
to fulfill the heart's desires.

Summer times all eyes bright,
winter's hazy clouds is past,
nothing passes by scarcely unseen,
lust displays its multi needs,
in all areas of life.

The earthly brightness reflects the skies,
the radiance of the stars increase,
the whole universe swells with busting beauty,
all gives combined glory to God,
sun, moon and stars, near distant and far,
beams the universe like a distant diamond.

Raptured in a quiet summer night,
in exclusion of all emotions,
steadfastly gazing out into space,
observing the beauty of the universe,
the quiet songs the universe sings,
songs of the universe,
amplify loudly in my ears,
the stars respond with beaming reflect,
their brightness fills the earth.

Life Is a Breath

Life is a gift,
short as a ziff
dub as a vapor,
classified as a breath,
meant for eternal time,
but here comes a serpent,
carries a virus,
the deadly virus of sin.

Strike with a deadly sting,
injected the virus of sin,
life is infected,
contaminated and corrupted,
life is cut short, by zillions of fractions,
of what it was intended to be.

No name could be found,
to describe life's short span,
as life is a gift, short as a ziff,
dub as a vapor,
starts as a germ, ends with a worm.

The City of Brooklyn

Brooklyn, Brooklyn, City of Brooklyn,
no city like the City of Brooklyn,
a city within the greatest city,
second in size among its boroughs
of five,
gleaming with geographical excellence
and beauty,
its borders are marked by highways,
bridges, rivers and sea,
not to mention its many bays and harbours.

Brooklyn, Brooklyn, City of Brooklyn,
a city open and welcome to all,
whether near or from afar,
cool and comely, marred and scarred,
come by bus, train, plane, or car,
or flee from a place most ravaged
by war,
a city opens with welcome arms,
some welcome one here, welcome
two there,
but good old Brooklyn welcomes all.

Brooklyn, Brooklyn, City of Brooklyn,
a thousand streets is not enough,
in number, name to seal the count,
of the many streets of Brooklyn,
highways tunnels, bridges, skies,
waterways and railways,
therefore its ways are of ultimate
possibilities.

Brooklyn a city most convenient,
most necessities at right hand reach,
accessibilities at thy left hand reach,
from six to six, twelve to twelve,
sunrise to sunrise,
the lights of Brooklyn,
never cease from shining.

Brooklyn, a city most compact together,
its population most densely thick,
not much place to lay a brick,
yet enough place to heal the sick,
all things are in abundance
to choose from and take your pick.

With working hands the people goes out,
as sure as the rising sun
in numbers can hardly be counted,
productive, sincere and ambitious,
their hands are established,
they make the city glad,
their children healthy and well.

Brooklyn, Brooklyn, City of Brooklyn,
place of music and art,
great number of institutions,
the people go to the high places for learning,
their knowledge increases
they are made bright and display
self-confidence and pride.

City of Brooklyn,
where grass is green, the gardens
kept and manicured,
they prune and dress the trees
and guide their branches,
humble city for the eyes to see,
the reflection of a people of color
and race,
my dwelling place my feet are
planted,
no other city like the
City of Brooklyn.

All Nations Pray for Peace

Let all nations pray for peace,
that all conflict and strife may cease,
and all people might relief from their grief,
that engulfs the nations of the Middle East.

The blood of adults and children stains the street,
people mauled to bits and pieces like helpless beasts,
bodies and rubbles pile in heaps,
behind the dark veil the devil feast,
humans' flesh and blood his favorite meat.

The stigma for life has come the least,
even for those sit on high seats,
some wonder why even bother to eat,
to face more days of life's down beat.

Where's the virtue of life once so sweet,
we sowed and reap the abundance of our wheat,
in marketplace we should make profit and greet,
retire home rest and sweet sleep.

Atrocities, deceptions, lies and deceit,
has weakened and wobbled the muscled feet,
with no future no past caused many to leap,
even from highest to most mighty deep,
with no regard for their little ones that creep.

Let's all stand in the gap, praying for those that weep,
that hearts and mind transforms to humility
and make meek,
in the end the children say, life is grand, happy,
wide open and sweet.

Maiden in Essence

Maidens in essence, carries no laden,
bears no children, free of all burden,
uniquely fair in their own way
their beauty like the morning's sunray,
that men rise early to see.

Their body firm yet tender,
skin soft like velvet and shines like fine oil,
their hands and feet, fingers and toes,
tall and neatly fit,
their breasts like seal fountains of goodly juice,
and like a pillow to rest your head,
odor like fresh mountains' fragrance.

They be decked in bright apparel
latest fashion go display
love flowers and sing for leisure,
they go their way with songs
and congregate with their own kind,
looking like flowers in kind and beauty.

They set not their heart to quick marry,
neither go look for princes,
they keep themselves in order,
they despise vain communications,
and go to the places of learning,
maidens in essence,
prepare today for the women tomorrow.

The Spirit and the Life

The body is the vehicle where indwellers
the spirit and the life.
To be absent from the body,
the life in its spirit form
returns to the great him,
that make both life and spirit.

The birds of the air the beast of the field
the fishes of the sea and all creeping things has life,
but mankind have both life
and spirit, even the spirit of life.

When life comes forth in a body
it dies to the flesh,
that, at the end of the reign of the flesh
life in its spirit form must live again.

We always wonder why we die,
but we must all die,
so, our children, and our children's children may live.
Therefore the death of all nations is the birth of all
generations.

High Flying Geese

High fly the geese,
over land and sea.
Their journey hardly cease,
they hardly get to sleep.
From the greatest to the least,
uncles, aunts, nephews and nieces.

In jungles they never rest their feet,
fearing predators and wild beasts.
Savagely hunt them, make great feast,
tears them to bits piece by piece.

They keep their feathers free from grease,
never got stuck in narrow crease.
Their way they go in unity and peace,
ever so often their numbers increase.

The Joy of Children

Children are like shining stars,
The reflection of light in the dark,
Our hope in a void place,
Where children abound there is life and light,
They are like the stars of heaven,
In likeness beauty and numbers.

Children are like flowers,
A hundred blended colors,
Freshly blooms in the morning's brightness,
With joyous singing, playing and laughter,
Gray clouds makes way for a sunny day,
The sun smiles bright as they make its day.

A warm hug, a tender touch,
Hopeful eyes a trusting look,
A malady parent's urge to live,
So trusting and innocent,
Their lives are in our hands,
Clear mind, clean heart,
Change the enemy's mind,
Countenance of peace,
Chase despair away.

Friend of the morning, songs of the day,
Rest in the evening, lights of all time,
The gentle sleep in the quiet night,
So are our children in all their attributes.

Children make the womb rejoice,
And heals the barren womb,
A home without a child abides,
Like food without the taste of salt,
Wealth, riches, fame in a home,
True happiness comes when a child is born,
Children are the parents of all generations.

Pray for America

Pray for continued peace for America
Its countless showering blessings
will always stay,
its pastures will always rich and green,
fresh running streams which with
full strength flows.

Let its city gates be tightly guarded,
by the flaming swords from above,
its borders keeps from sea to sea,
so adversaries will always let her be.

Her clear blue skies and bright patchy clouds,
reflect with heavenly brightness,
keep by power of flashing lightning,
and roaring thunder from heaven above.

Her trees be tall and strong,
racing to greet the bright sunlight,
her hills fresh and green,
fresh water trickles down mountainside,
rain clouds regular descent is seen,
white clouds cap the mountain's top.

Its wilderness thirst always quenched,
from the heavenly sprinkled dew,
the night wind soothes parched deserted land,
all wild beast freely roams.

Let enemies and tyrants be converted,
from hate and evil
to enduring love and peace,
sharing wisdom, knowledge and goodwill,
for all mankind,
grasping total orderly freedom
and countless privileges,
that America freely gives to all.

My Battles

My battles I fought, I won not one,
Only live to fight again,
Daily constant fighting on
Fighting the struggles of life.

No fancy hero's welcome home,
No wounded body, nor broken bones,
No tombstone heads a silent grave,
No name engraves a monument.

Quick lived heroes are great warriors indeed,
Quench the fire of the battle's fury,
But they that stay the battles are greater,
Even crushed its ugly head.

The daily toiling not much joy brings,
Songs of bitter sweet I sing,
Heart not merry like conquering kings,
Who drink and make merry,
When battles are won.

Fighting, fighting, day by day,
Hoping one day victory come my way,
So to myself I may one day say,
The battles I've fought, I've won them all,
The war is over, I go no more may day,
The raging storm is past,
I stay the battle to the end.
I triumph in victory.

King of Kings

God the father, God the son, God the holy spirit,
God the creator of all things,
the only reason to exist and to live.

He is the fragrance of life,
the warmth of the sun, the clearness of our day,
the way through the dark,
the ultimate remedy for the most excruciating,
physical, spiritual, mental, psychological,
and all diverse pain.

He is our place in the rock,
the smoke from my chimney,
the spice in my food, healer of my wound,
his blood the only antibiotic,
for the virus of sin,
and maintaining antidote for sin.

He is the reflections of all true smiles,
the songs in my mouth, my laughter and my joy,
our grips on solid ice,
He is the river that flows through all cities
the only sword against the most powerful,
invasions of evil.

His breaths are the blue mist,
of the morning's valley dew,
the lights of his eyes are the beams,
of the morning's golden sunrays,
author of my divinity,
source of all foods
to whom all universal attributes go forth,
King of Kings and Lord of Lords,
Jesus Christ Son of God,
Reign for ever and ever, Amen.

Aging

When we are grown and are aging,
bit by bit and stage by stage,
youth and favor passing away,
looking back over past days,
glancing through portraits page by page,
wondering what might be our fate,
even if we might lose our mate.

What it might be to start a new date,
depend on the physical and emotional state,
because of age if we might look
and feel great,
if we will rise up early or wake too late,
or be able to wash mugs, spoons,
pans, and plates,
in a long line if we might be able to wait.

One must remember they are not alone
in their time of birth,
we were accompanied by millions,
therefore we are many far and near,
aging together in same likeness and fashion,
some minutes older, some days,
some weeks, months, years,
we grow together, we age together.

We might be strangers one to another,
consider our personal state and give thanks,
it could be worse as it is with some,
millions came not half as far,
we full, we fill, we fulfill our gaps
stage by stage in each different ways.

Remember, we were a generation
that brings great joy at birth,
even to them that behold us as
second and third generation,
so we behold the same or more.

We were seeds sown, germinate
and tenderly transplant in the
display of life,
we run our journey, withered and fading
we go our way,
to a life beyond this life they say,
we never grow old but forever young,
like a child throughout eternity.

Women Are Like Flowers

Women are like flowers,
appears weak in power,
adorned in different colors,
reflect in multifashions and styles,
their beauty is endless,
renewed every day,
their teeth are white,
their hair in style,
quench men's thirst,
with only a smile.

Their steps are in line,
their chest held high,
their eyes so bright,
as if there is no night.
Men lost their sight,
focused with all might,
see nothing so bright,
like women like flower,
different in color.

Their adversaries are few,
we haven't got a clue,
who wanna make them into beef stew
when falls in the wrong queue.

They gave birth fill the earth,
their womb contain life.
Harmless dove, humble sheep,
serpent stings she crushed its head.
A man can do without many,
But men can't do without any.

Mistake to Beefsteak

Turn your mistakes into beefsteak
do it timely without any haste.
Too much haste can make big waste
which could throw you into bad state.
It's better to be late than to sit and wait
try your best not to miss your date.

Writing every day on the same old slate
you know that really upset Mrs. Kate.
Careful not to make yourself a bate
you may certainly turn off your mate.

The place she came from name Mount Tate
every high hill she sees she hates.
Her father's name is Mr. Nate.

Used to sell stockpiles of crate
his pretty house has a big white gate.
That is why his name is so great.

In Time of Love

In time of love my hunger flees,
food has no taste that I may eat,
love substitutes my appetite,
deprives my urge to eat,
where is the taste for food,
that I may eat and be filled.

Love is blind you never see fault,
love makes the strong weak,
and the mighty fall,
love makes the pompous pliable,
causes the heart to ponder.

At the presence of love,
you can hear the heart beats,
as first kiss is sweet,
unable to keep your seat,
'cause love sweeter than choice meat.

Love chooses most feeble strings,
to bind and lead the powerful,
love is predominant,
its insults are gratified,
its no's are yes.

Rejection finds exultation,
walk many miles to get one smile,
its wounds so deep only a painless scratch,
passion so tender love covers all,
love like subdued a fortified city
with a warm welcome
and a true, bright smile.

Praise Jahovia

Praise Jahovia bless his name,
from whom all blessings flow,
glory praise, and honor to his name,
through all eternity he is the same.

Wealth and gain from him all came,
gives they him whom ever he please,
clean and obedient heart he pleasures,
and values more than silver and gold.

Some he keeps low they may not go,
beyond his boundary set,
many may come and pass them by,
make them night and day to sigh.

Your life may be like bitter sweet,
that still say not he isn't all fame,
lead us by the guide of providence,
all glory to his name amen.

I Miss You

I remember when we used to play
in the meadow on spring times,
we would hunt turtledoves
and wild rabbits too,
eat lots of fruits and hear the birds sing
but now you have gone away,
but now you have gone away.

The grasses still growing,
and the flowers still blooming,
the waters still flowing,
an the sun still shining
and, how much I miss you
because you have gone away,
because you have gone away.

You promised me you would come
when spring time is near
'cause I am so longing
to see you my dear
because you have gone away,
because you have gone away.

I am so longing to hold you
and touch you,
to look in your eyes
and tell you I love you,
to hold your hands
and to walk with you,
but now you have gone away,
but now you have gone away.

At the Presence of the Lord

At the presence of the Lord,
a great radiant light goeth forth,
the darkness flees and be no more,
the earth trembles, the seas roar,
the waters, boil and dissipate,
a great wind goeth forth,
the oceans flee the great depths are exposed.

At the presence of the Lord,
a fire goeth forth with intense heat
it burns, it devours, it purges and it purifies,
the mountains melts, the high places are thrown down,
the earth gushed open its belly exposes.

At the presence of the Lord,
the whole universe raptures in the nostril
of judgment, for judgment.

Every knee shall bow for all is come to judgment,
time and all is passed away,
except the purged and the purified,
at the presence of the Lord,
at the presence of the Lord.

Young and Selfish

When you were young
you grasped self and pride,
in thoughts deeds and will,
in your self you said,
I know it all and well,
you did what looks and feels good
in your own eyes.

Grieved parents and hurt friends,
despised councils of the elders,
broke rules and find it amuse
discredited right and called it wrong,
embraced wrongs and say it's right,
played the fool and say it's cool.

You grown much more than a child,
much less than a man,
defeated by your own habitual practices,
wounded, bruises battered and blue,
despicable, desolate and debased,
all your past returns to you.

In your deep place of solitariness,
you cried out from your place
of desolation,
set free by a mighty and gentle hand,
God lifts up his countenance
upon thee,
and gives you his perfect peace,
you embrace life with a different perspective,
value the council of the elders,
publish obedience, purged from selfishness,
leave self open for positive duties.

A Woman I Know

A woman I know from a long time ago
not many women like her I know
I constantly watched her as she grows
from a teenager to an adult folk
her fairness and beauty not a joke
her ways of life one day at a time

this woman I know so loyal and true
have a heart so natural and kind
this woman I know was all men's choice
choice to choose over all or most
all men's heart pants for her love
even to get one of her smiles and converse

her conversations are encouraging
her smiles are uplifting
her feet walk not for vain things
neither chasten the world
in lending hand she gives it all
lift them up that cast down low
to the poor and needy she never says no
always welcome with open arms

this woman I know from a long time ago
children she bore of her own
with eagle's eyes she watch them grow
on eagle's wings she bear them all
with eagle's strength she mounts up high
to the cleft in the rocks where she abides

she is a lady a mother a sister a queen and a friend
a vineyard's main vine a special flower
a garden at the foot of a blue mountain
a quiet stream trickles by
covered by a mist at night
damp with the morning's dew
lightened by the rising golden sunrays

combined fragrance of angel's breath
and angel's spilled perfumes
this woman I know from a long time ago
she is my most beloved wife
God bless you a woman I know
from a long time ago.

Greed

Greed drips the fountain dried,
so all my neighbor's cattle died,
greed have no pride,
greed have no guide,
greed choose no side.

Greed said all sides are mine,
and what's thine are mine,
no one else shall abide,
only me myself and I.

If There Was No America

If there was no America,
How great and void a space would be,
In exclusion of a continent.
If there was no America,
How deep and dark the vast abyss,
Would likely stay unfathomed.

If there was no America,
The absence of a nation great,
Where freedom forever reign,
In the time of harvest much gain,
Barns overflowing much wheat and grain,
Freely gives to nations in hunger and pain,
Where crops fail because of much strife,
And lack of rain.

If there was no America,
Where would be a place for refuge?
And a mighty wing to shadows,
All nations fleeing oppress,
Displace their hunger,
And quench their bitter thirst.

If there was no America,
Who would execute the order of the world?
Challenge most mighty tyrants,
Break their solid bond of power,
Chasten subdue them as they flee,
Loose all chains and set their captives free.

Or who would cease the warrior's fury,
And their entire flagrant firebrand,
Put out their raging fires,
Deprive their appetite for blood.

If there was no America,
Who would plant a monument,
On the mountains above the earth?
Or who would behold a making star,
As it births from its celestial womb,
Or who would fathom the mighty deep,
And know the springs of the seas,
Reveal her secret parts,
Even explore her hidden caves,
Glide the ocean's bed.

If there was no America,
Who would streak and shadow the skies?
With chariots like rolling thunder,
Thrust by flaming fire,
Send some among the distant stars.

Who could race the day that passed?
Start at the setting sun,
Like lightning overtook the noonday,
Deprives the sun its long night rest,
Like rising from the western horizon,
And so descend beyond the east.

Let America be told she have some
Searching to do,
Find its wound, wash, clean, dress
And be healed,
That God may continue on thee shed his grace,
A humble hand he maketh mighty,
With a flaming sword,
Founding fathers children of pilgrimages,
Hands of the laborers,
Make a nation strong,
Land of the free, home of the brave,
God bless America.

Mighty Ships

As our mighty ships set sail the seas,
They not sustained by wind alone,
That sometimes toss them to and fro,
But by mega force from source
Of flaming fire,
Caused by intense heat.
Such mighty power sustain every hour,
Exceed ten thousand horses' power.

Quick speed and mega force,
Give respect to the mighty deep,
They see the storm and know its name,
Even before it's fast approaching.

They face the storm and brace its wind,
Surf the mighty waves,
Fear not its frightening war clouds,
But journey through its darkness,
Enduring the raging sea.

Go ye go ye o mighty ships
The storm is ceased at last,
Go ye quick and mighty vessel
The ocean's fury is past,
Go ye go ye mighty ships,
Black clouds wring their garments white,
Hang them patchy in the sky to dry,
Go ye go ye mighty ships,
The sun's shine make thy burden light,
Go ye go ye o mighty ships,
Sustain her laidens and occupants,
Safe to her destined harbor.

Wipe My Falling Tears

When my days are filled with sorrow,
and all tha songs gone from my mouth,
joy and laughter penalize me,
my byways full of thorns,
my brooks run low and dry up,
flowers fade and bloom no more,
all the summer birds migrated,
and the sparrows sing no more.

Friends and neighbors all despise me,
as rumor spreads from sea to sea,
my humble ways they fail to see,
that I despise all bad deeds,
I lift my face to the sky and cry,
I say the truth and tell no lie,
with open heart I pray and cry,
to thee alone who rules from on high.

He wipes my falling tears,
dries with tender care,
my burden he gladly bears,
remove my trembling fear,
I'll never find a friend so dear,
Jesus wipe my falling tears.

Now I find peace and comfort,
In his territorial realm of peace,
Joyful heartsongs and laughter,
Tears dispelled and dried away,
Raptured in eternal refuge,
Mountains move and cast asunder,
From sea to sea the far horizon,
Endless place belongs to me.

Prudent with a Gun

Guns can be deadly and evil,
Can make children frightened and feeble,
It's a favorite tool of the devil,
Especially when in the hands of a rebel.

It serves its rightful purpose,
Keep the peace and maintains law,
Breaks all tyrants' grips of bondage,
Destroys their rule of jingoism,
And sets their opposing captives free.

Guns are instruments of death,
You never say bet,
Its bullets are always set,
A gun is not a tool to play with or pet,
A gun in presence makes one fret,
One shot and there goes your breath.

Guns kill and murder many
Daughters and sons,
The killers are thrown in the slum,
And there their future is forever done,
At the presence of a gun,
The doors of death swings wide open,
Inside is dark, lonely, and cold.

Legacy of the Ages

Our first father in the flesh left us all
a legacy,
inheritance most grievous to bear,
flows through the bloodline of the ages,
as the story told in the pages.

The flesh displays its agonies
most when it starts to fade away,
the voice responds with ceaseless groaning,
from the heart's silent moaning.
Reflects the face with sad atoning,
From life's harsh and constant pounding.

All tribes and nations bleeding,
Yet higher powers interceding,
Mercies for mankind's needing,
Daily bread of life for mankind's feeding.

Life was not meant to be this way,
But a deceiver stole the key,
A liar, a thief, a murderer indeed,
By sooting deceit and garbled fabrication,
Twist the truth into a lie,
And a lie displaces the truth.

The eyes of the first parents were open,
Stripped naked by the deceiver's lie,
Fall into a deceptive interpretation,
Man has utilitized his freedom of
choice to choose privilege.

Transition his eternal life privilege,
To a deceiver,
Driven by jealousy and pride,
Not for silver, nor for gold,
Neither for a price well paid,
But for free, even for nothing,

But in exchange for eternal death and
Damnation,
So make him the certified one,
Having the power of death in his hands,
Over man's children and children's children,
A legacy of the ages.

Flashing lightning, thunder rolling,
Creation groans, Earth moans,
Ready to be rolled up like a scroll,
Pass away and be no more,
But out of a frightening dark cloud and
Rumbling earthquake,
A moving force called mercy intrepid,
Having indomitable power,
Launched from the bottomless pit of hell.

Driven and powered by innocent blood for fuel,
Its inscription and trademark was mercy,
All commotion ceased, all returned to peace,
In the beginning a temporary price was paid
By innocent blood, of a sheep,
In the end the eternal price was bought and
Paid for by supernatural innocent blood
For eternal life redemption.